Beginner's German

Copyright © Lexis

All rights reserved. No part of this publication
prior written permission from the Copyright holder.

Front cover photo by Anna Tis

No. 1
Numbers

Across
3. six
4. three
5. eighteen
6. four
7. ten
8. seventy
10. ninety
13. two
14. twelve
16. nine
17. eleven
18. forty
19. nineteen

Down
1. fourteen
2. eight
3. seven
5. eighty
8. sixty
9. fifty
11. sixteen
12. thirty
15. five

No. 2
Days and Months

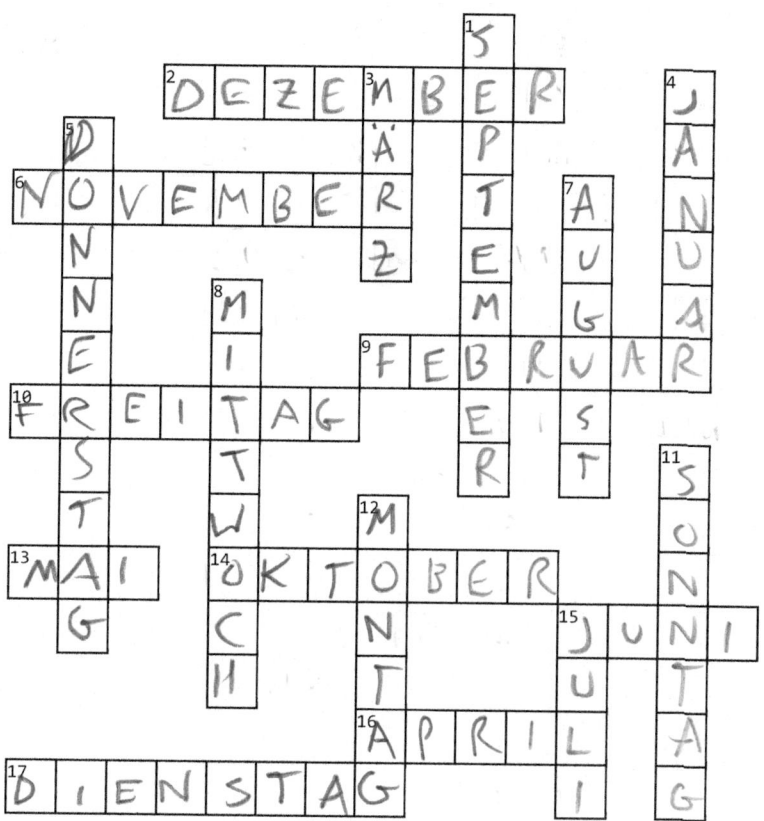

Across
2. December
6. November
9. February
10. Friday
13. May
14. October
15. June
16. April
17. Tuesday

Down
1. September
3. March
4. January
5. Thursday
7. August
8. Wednesday
11. Sunday
12. Monday
15. July

No. 3
Animals

Across
2. cat
3. spider
7. fish
9. deer
10. frog
11. dog
13. octopus
17. ant
19. camel
20. bee
23. bird
24. pig

Down
1. rabbit
4. horse
5. lizard
6. animal
8. chicken
12. goat
13. crab
14. monkey
15. whale
16. goose
18. swan
21. duck
22. cow

No. 4
The Body

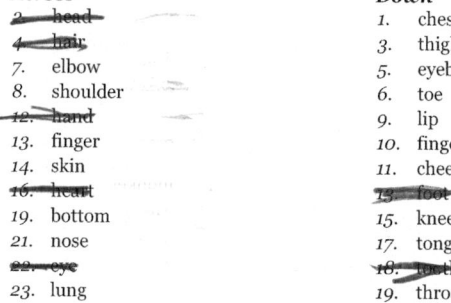

Across
2. head
4. hair
7. elbow
8. shoulder
12. hand
13. finger
14. skin
16. heart
19. bottom
21. nose
22. eye
23. lung

Down
1. chest
3. thigh
5. eyebrow
6. toe
9. lip
10. finger nail
11. cheek
13. foot
15. knee
17. tongue
18. tooth
19. throat
20. leg

No. 5
Food

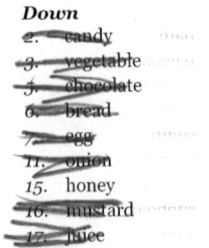
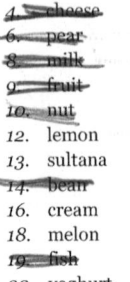

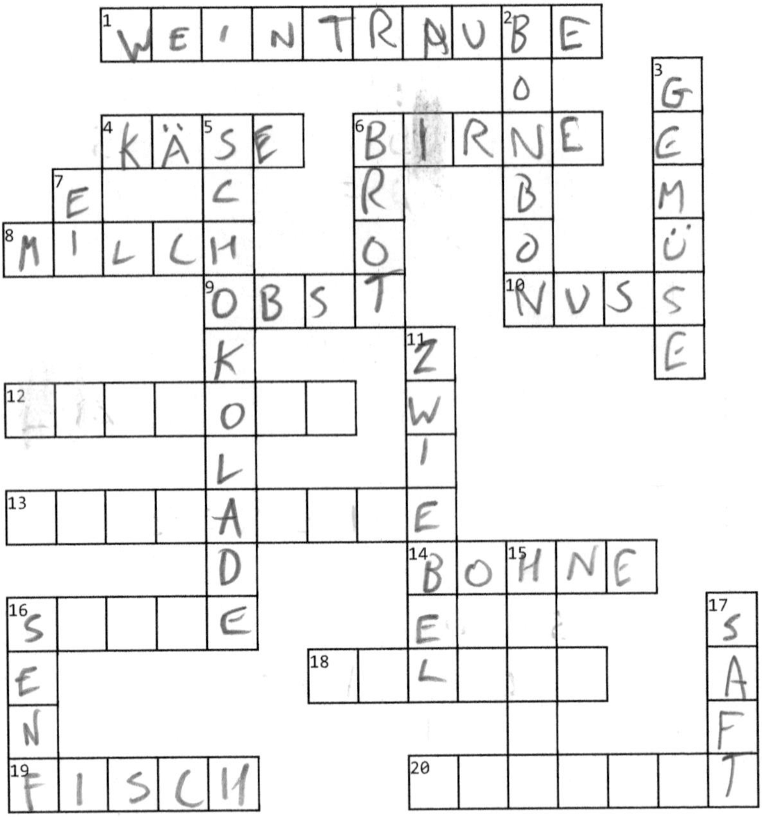

Across
1. grape
4. cheese
6. pear
8. milk
9. fruit
10. nut
12. lemon
13. sultana
14. bean
16. cream
18. melon
19. fish
20. yoghurt

Down
2. candy
3. vegetable
5. chocolate
6. bread
7. egg
11. onion
15. honey
16. mustard
17. juice

No. 6
The Home

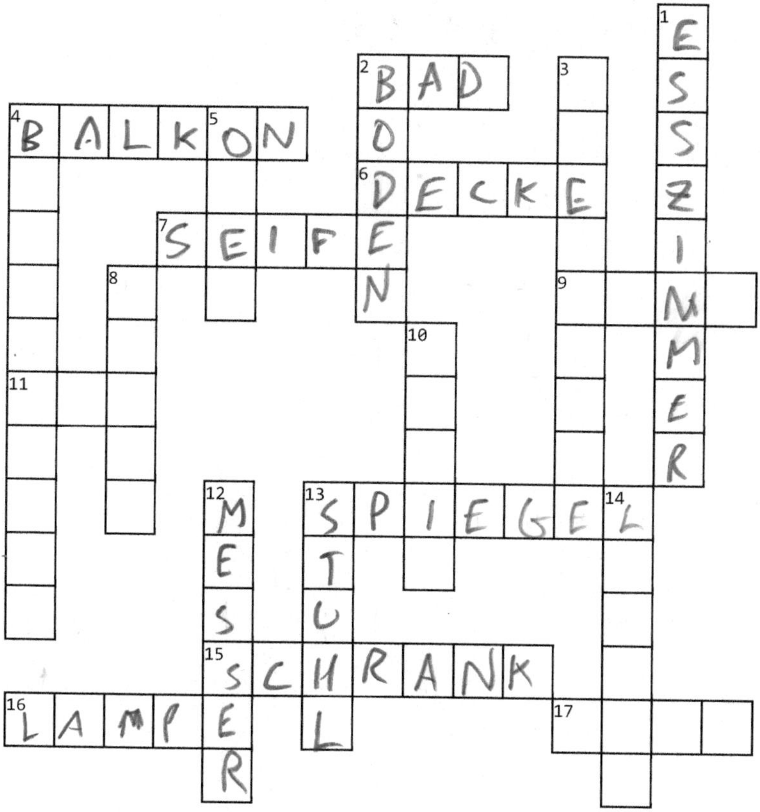

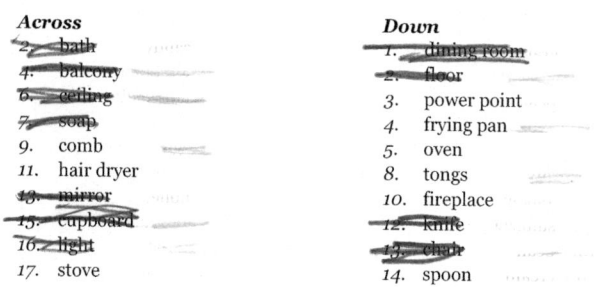

Across
- 2. bath
- 4. balcony
- 6. ceiling
- 7. soap
- 9. comb
- 11. hair dryer
- 13. mirror
- 15. cupboard
- 16. light
- 17. stove

Down
- 1. dining room
- 2. floor
- 3. power point
- 4. frying pan
- 5. oven
- 8. tongs
- 10. fireplace
- 12. knife
- 13. chair
- 14. spoon

No. 7
Clothes and Colors

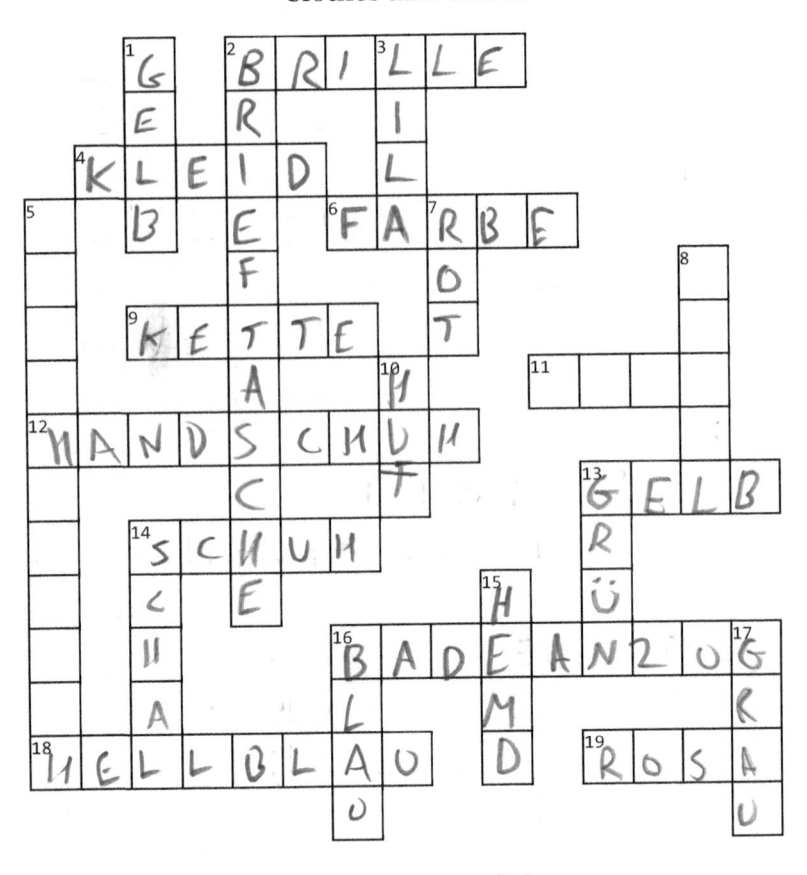

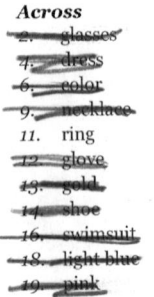

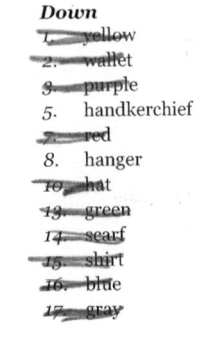

Crossword grid filled in:

- 1 Down: GELB
- 2 Across: BRILLE; 2 Down: BRIEFTASCHE
- 3 Down: LILA
- 4 Across: KLEID
- 5 Down: (blank)
- 6 Across: FARBE
- 7 Down: ROT
- 8 Down: (blank)
- 9 Across: KETTE
- 10 Down: HUT
- 11 Across: RING
- 12 Across: HANDSCHUH
- 13 Across: GELB; 13 Down: GRÜN
- 14 Across: SCHUH; 14 Down: SCHAL
- 15 Down: HEMD
- 16 Across: BADEANZUG; 16 Down: BLAU
- 17 Down: GRAU
- 18 Across: HELLBLAU
- 19 Across: ROSA

Across
- 2. glasses
- 4. dress
- 6. color
- 9. necklace
- 11. ring
- 12. glove
- 13. gold
- 14. shoe
- 16. swimsuit
- 18. light blue
- 19. pink

Down
- 1. yellow
- 2. wallet
- 3. purple
- 5. handkerchief
- 7. red
- 8. hanger
- 10. hat
- 13. green
- 14. scarf
- 15. shirt
- 16. blue
- 17. gray

No. 8
People

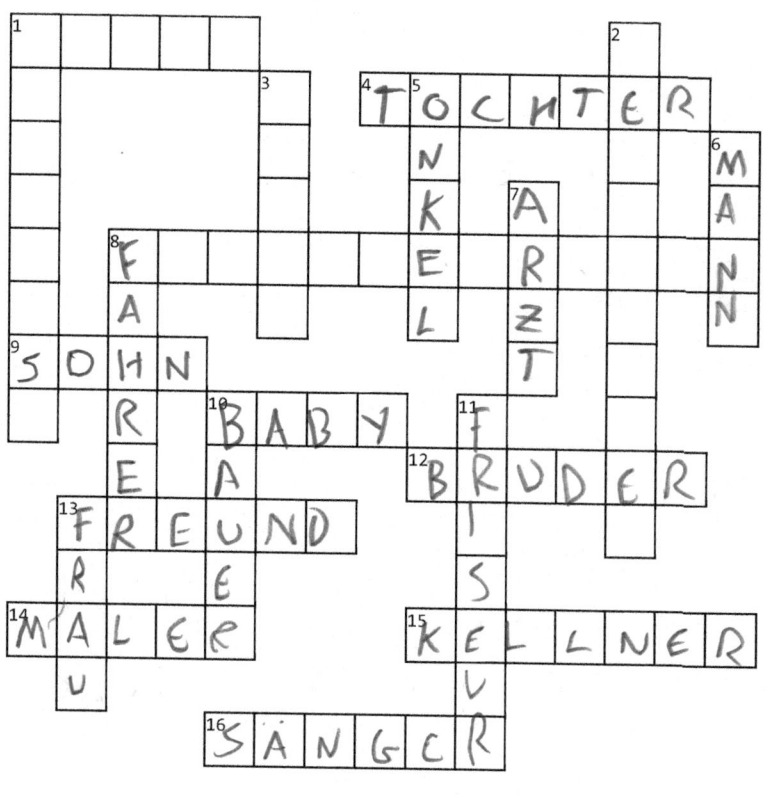

Across
1. pilot
4. daughter
8. fireman
9. son
10. baby
12. brother
13. friend
14. painter
15. waiter
16. singer

Down
1. policeman
2. mechanic
3. hunter
5. uncle
6. man
7. doctor
8. driver
10. farmer
11. hairdresser
13. woman

No. 9
Actions

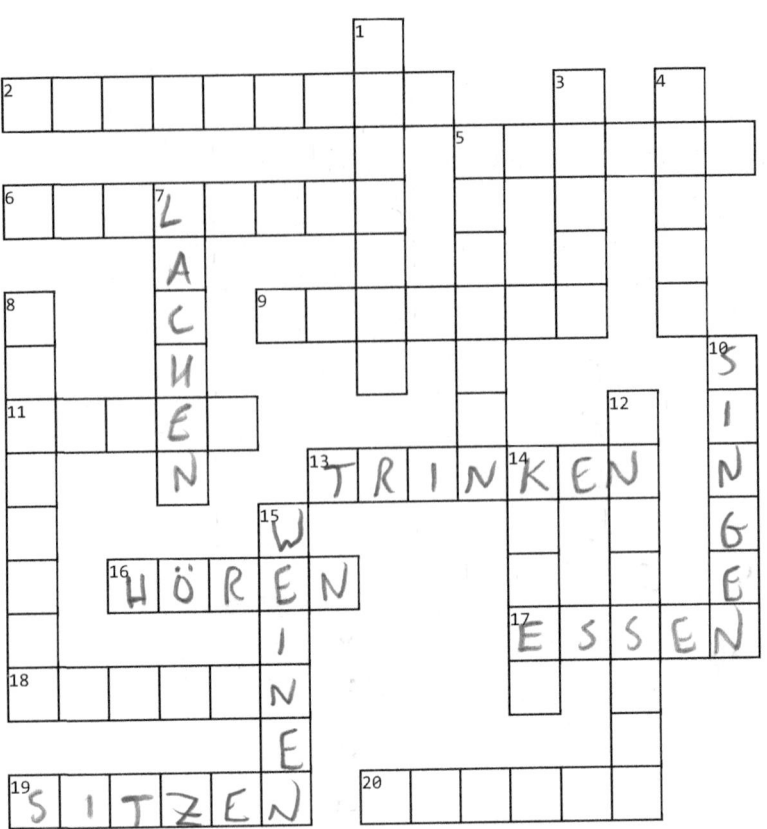

Across
2. to shake
5. to lie
6. to punch
9. to smell
11. to shout
13. to drink
16. to listen
17. to eat
18. to sneeze
19. to sit
20. to kick

Down
1. to blink
3. to talk
4. to walk
5. to smile
7. to laugh
8. to stretch
10. to sing
12. to touch
14. to kneel
15. to cry

No. 10
The Outdoors

Across
1. coast
4. lightning
5. plain
8. storm
10. sea
11. frost
13. flood
14. lake
15. forest
16. cloudy
19. fog
20. rain
21. rainbow

Down
1. cold
2. river
3. waterfall
6. weather
7. island
9. rainy
12. hill
13. cliff
15. cloud
17. ocean
18. mountain

No. 11
Numbers

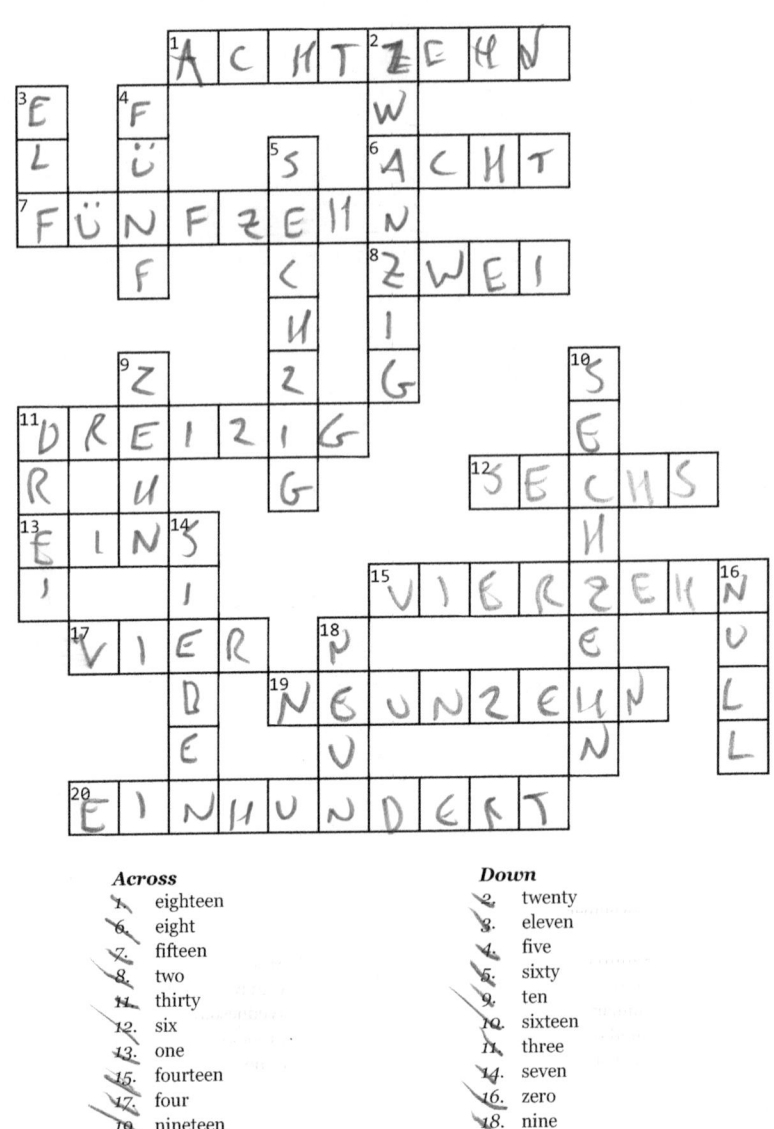

Across
1. eighteen
6. eight
7. fifteen
8. two
11. thirty
12. six
13. one
15. fourteen
17. four
19. nineteen
20. one hundred

Down
2. twenty
3. eleven
4. five
5. sixty
9. ten
10. sixteen
11. three
14. seven
16. zero
18. nine

No. 12
Days and Months

Across
1. Tuesday
4. November
5. April
8. Saturday
10. March
12. January
13. Sunday
14. August

Down
1. Thursday
2. July
3. September
6. May
7. Friday
9. Wednesday
11. Monday
12. June

No. 13
Animals

Across
1. fish
5. cow
6. monkey
8. horse
9. camel
11. pig
13. bee
15. rabbit
18. cat
19. lizard
20. duck

Down
2. snake
3. deer
4. crab
6. ant
7. spider
10. animal
12. chicken
13. bear
14. goat
15. octopus
16. dog
17. sheep

No. 14
The Body

Across
4. hair
6. stomach
8. cheek
9. toe
10. thigh
13. tongue
16. chest
17. ear
18. throat
20. back
21. heart
22. skin
23. lung

Down
1. nose
2. arm
3. finger
4. bottom
5. knee
7. eyebrow
11. hip
12. foot
13. tooth
14. face
15. head
19. leg
21. hand

No. 15
Food

Across
3. bread
7. mustard
8. soup
10. noodle
13. milk
15. juice
17. pea
18. meat
20. tomato
21. cream

Down
1. bean
2. cheese
4. apple
5. cauliflower
6. pasta
9. vegetable
10. nut
11. egg
12. capsicum
14. pepper
16. melon
19. salt

No. 16
The Home

Across
3. toaster
4. floor
7. oven
9. fence
10. hallway
12. table
14. shower
17. cupboard
18. garden
19. knife

Down
1. balcony
2. alarm clock
5. soap
6. tap
8. handle
11. chair
13. sponge
14. blanket
15. tongs
16. wall

No. 17
Clothes and Colors

Across
3. black
5. red
7. light blue
9. yellow
11. belt
12. dress
14. blue
17. coat
18. sock
19. glove
20. color

Down
1. scarf
2. necklace
4. pink
6. skirt
7. pants
8. hanger
9. gold
10. wallet
13. purple
15. jeans
16. shirt
18. shoe

No. 18
People

Across
7. painter
8. man
9. sister
12. boy
14. soldier
17. mother
18. brother
19. doctor

Down
1. hairdresser
2. woman
3. artist
4. farmer
5. grandmother
6. dentist
10. uncle
11. daughter
13. friend
14. son
15. aunt
16. baby

No. 19
Actions

Across
1. to hold
4. to talk
8. to point
9. to push
10. to stand
12. to grip
14. to smile
16. to cry
17. to eat
18. to bend

Down
2. to kick
3. to sit
5. to sneeze
6. to turn
7. to sing
10. to punch
11. to touch
12. to walk
13. to kneel
15. to listen

No. 20
The Outdoors

Across
1. sea
3. storm
7. cloud
9. cliff
11. island
12. mountain
13. cave
16. forest
18. fog
20. plain
22. cloudy
23. cold

Down
2. rain
4. valley
5. lake
6. desert
8. coast
9. flood
10. snow
14. hill
15. ocean
16. wind
17. river
19. lightning
21. hot

No. 21
Numbers

Across
1. twenty
3. eighty
4. ten
8. fifty
10. fourteen
11. one
13. zero
14. seventeen
17. nine
18. twelve
19. forty

Down
2. eight
3. eighteen
5. seven
6. six
7. nineteen
9. five
10. four
12. ninety
15. eleven
16. two

No. 22
Days and Months

Across
1. Thursday
3. September
5. January
6. Friday
8. Wednesday
9. April
10. October
11. August

Down
1. December
2. Tuesday
3. Sunday
4. March
5. June
6. February
7. Monday
8. May

No. 23
Animals

Across
2. butterfly
5. chicken
6. animal
9. octopus
11. rabbit
12. ant
14. horse
15. frog
16. cat
17. spider
18. whale
19. cow
20. bee

Down
1. deer
2. snake
3. mouse
4. duck
7. dog
8. goose
10. sheep
11. crab
12. monkey
13. turkey
15. fish

No. 24
The Body

Across
1. ear
6. back
7. eye
9. knee
11. lung
12. stomach
14. chest
16. arm
17. cheek
18. heart
21. hand
22. thumb
23. jaw

Down
2. skin
3. hip
4. leg
5. face
8. tongue
9. head
10. elbow
12. mouth
13. nose
15. shoulder
19. tooth
20. foot

No. 25
Food

Across
4. tomato
5. carrot
6. fruit
8. pasta
9. pumpkin
11. rice
12. mustard
15. pear
16. bread
17. vegetable
19. yoghurt
20. noodle
21. onion

Down
1. cream
2. melon
3. juice
7. sauce
8. nut
9. cheese
10. soup
13. pea
14. fish
18. salt

No. 26
The Home

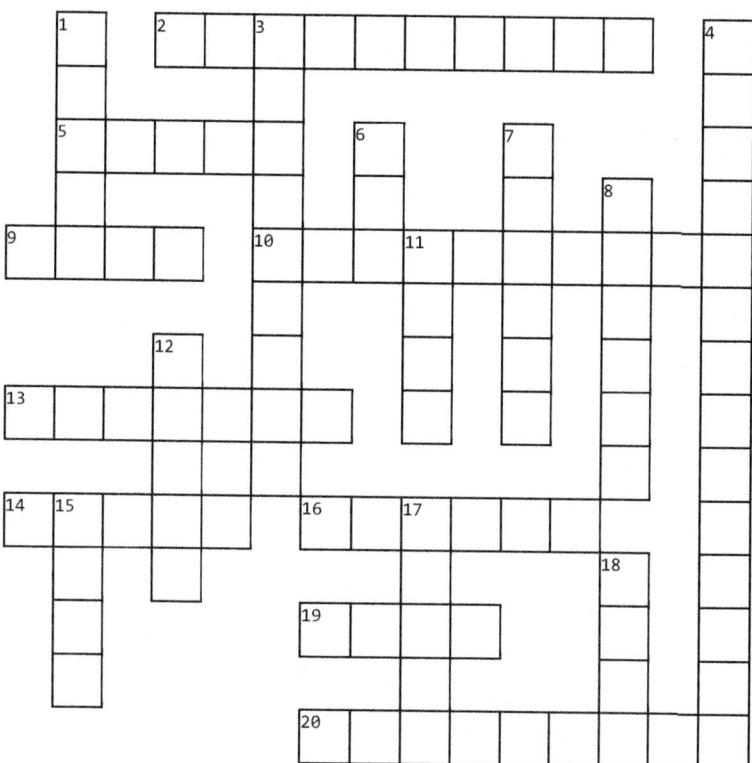

Across
2. tap
5. soap
9. stove
10. crib
13. home
14. floor
16. shower
19. hallway
20. trash can

Down
1. cup
3. power point
4. towel rack
6. hair dryer
7. garage
8. plate
11. roof
12. fork
15. oven
17. chair
18. comb

No. 27
Clothes and Colors

Across
2. necklace
4. glasses
5. red
8. green
11. gray
12. sneaker
13. coat
14. yellow
16. gold
17. shoe
18. color
19. purple
20. shirt

Down
1. white
2. dress
3. hat
4. wallet
5. ring
6. brown
7. pants
9. handbag
10. orange
15. hanger

No. 28
People

Across
1. man
5. soldier
7. hairdresser
9. brother
11. father
14. mother
16. singer
17. boy
18. doctor
19. plumber

Down
1. painter
2. son
3. driver
4. farmer
6. daughter
8. woman
10. fisherman
12. judge
13. lawyer
15. aunt

No. 29
Actions

Across
2. to dance
4. to yawn
5. to turn
8. to eat
10. to stand
11. to walk
12. to sing
16. to hold
17. to pull
18. to talk

Down
1. to rub
3. to wink
6. to kick
7. to point
9. to swim
12. to look
13. to run
14. to shout
15. to lick

No. 30
The Outdoors

Across
1. ocean
3. cave
5. lightning
6. cold
7. desert
12. cloud
13. island
14. cliff
15. hill
18. storm
19. flood
20. beach

Down
2. fog
3. hot
4. plain
7. cloudy
8. lake
9. sea
10. mountain
11. forest
12. wind
14. river
15. hail
16. frost
17. rain

No. 31
Numbers

Across
2. seventeen
5. fifteen
7. seventy
8. twenty
10. eight
12. thirteen
13. two
15. nineteen
17. sixteen
18. five

Down
1. eleven
3. one
4. three
6. fifty
9. one hundred
10. eighteen
11. four
12. thirty
13. ten
14. six
16. nine

No. 32
Days and Months

Across
1. July
6. Friday
7. March
8. August
11. October
13. September
14. December
16. Tuesday

Down
1. June
2. February
3. April
4. Saturday
5. January
9. Monday
10. November
12. Sunday
15. May

No. 33
Animals

Across
2. bear
6. fish
8. goose
9. cow
10. crab
12. monkey
15. cat
17. spider
19. whale
20. deer
21. chicken
22. pig

Down
1. octopus
3. snake
4. bee
5. duck
7. dog
10. camel
11. sheep
13. frog
14. ant
16. goat
18. mouse

No. 34
The Body

Across
2. hand
3. head
5. mouth
7. arm
8. throat
9. eye
10. nose
11. chest
12. elbow
15. knee
16. finger
19. lung
20. heart
21. skin

Down
1. tooth
3. body
4. stomach
6. thumb
8. bottom
11. leg
13. face
14. jaw
17. foot
18. toe

No. 35
Food

Across
2. pear
5. cucumber
9. potato
11. nut
12. soup
14. fish
15. sultana
16. flour
17. sauce
18. juice
19. rice
20. honey

Down
1. sugar
3. pasta
4. pumpkin
6. carrot
7. tomato
8. chicken
10. icecream
13. spinach
14. meat
15. cream

No. 36

The Home

Across
1. floor
4. chair
5. towel
7. slipper
10. trash can
13. roof
15. spoon
16. plate
17. hair dryer
18. mattress

Down
1. bath
2. home
3. comb
6. toaster
8. mirror
9. fireplace
11. lamp
12. sleep
14. saucepan
16. door

No. 37
Clothes and Colors

Across
1. watch
4. shorts
10. coat
11. bracelet
14. brown
15. scarf
16. gold
18. yellow
20. jeans
21. red
22. handkerchief
23. vest

Down
2. skirt
3. hat
5. shirt
6. ring
7. tie
8. pale green
9. color
12. glove
13. jacket
17. necklace
19. pants

No. 38
People

Across
2. policeman
5. brother
7. mother
12. sailor
13. lawyer
16. butcher
17. doctor
18. hairdresser
19. painter

Down
1. woman
3. uncle
4. soldier
5. baby
6. pilot
8. aunt
9. grandmother
10. waiter
11. singer
12. man
14. hunter
15. father

No. 39
Actions

Across
1. to bend
3. to kick
5. to blink
9. to point
10. to pull
11. to smell
14. to eat
15. to stand
16. to sing
17. to turn
18. to kneel

Down
2. to yawn
3. to dance
4. to drink
6. to laugh
7. to lie
8. to sit
11. to talk
12. to cry
13. to walk

No. 40
The Outdoors

Across
2. desert
3. beach
5. cave
7. flood
8. island
11. cloud
13. hail
15. lake
16. frost
17. fog
20. snow
21. rain

Down
1. cold
2. cloudy
4. valley
5. hill
6. volcano
7. plain
9. stormy
10. sea
12. coast
14. hot
16. river
18. lightning
19. mountain

No. 41
Numbers

Across
1. seven
2. five
4. eight
5. sixty
6. twelve
7. two
10. four
11. three
12. nineteen
14. eleven
15. twenty
17. ninety
18. nine

Down
1. six
3. fifteen
4. eighty
8. one
9. fifty
11. thirteen
13. ten
16. zero

No. 42
Days and Months

Across
3. November
5. January
7. Tuesday
9. Monday
10. February
11. Sunday
14. Wednesday
15. April
16. December

Down
1. Friday
2. Saturday
4. May
6. Thursday
8. August
9. March
12. October
13. July

No. 43
Animals

Across
6. chicken
7. ant
8. swan
9. dog
12. bear
14. sheep
15. fish
18. whale
19. pig
21. lizard
22. horse

Down
1. goose
2. bee
3. crab
4. deer
5. rabbit
10. frog
11. monkey
13. cow
14. spider
16. mouse
17. goat
20. duck

No. 44
The Body

Across
1. head
4. knee
5. chest
9. hair
10. throat
11. tongue
12. heart
15. finger
17. hand
18. elbow
20. thumb
22. tooth
23. stomach

Down
2. ear
3. jaw
4. body
6. shoulder
7. nose
8. cheek
12. hip
13. toe
14. lung
16. mouth
19. leg
21. arm

No. 45

Food

Across
2. cake
5. milk
6. butter
7. cauliflower
10. candy
11. meat
15. cheese
17. fish
18. noodle
19. tomato
20. sugar

Down
1. cabbage
3. egg
4. cucumber
5. melon
7. bread
8. flour
9. fruit
12. sauce
13. honey
14. cream
16. salt

No. 46
The Home

Across
1. light
6. garage
7. garden
10. fence
12. soap
14. table
15. window
17. roof
18. container
20. brush

Down
2. saucepan
3. oven
4. wall
5. tap
8. cup
9. plate
11. fork
13. crib
15. hair dryer
16. chair
19. door

No. 47
Clothes and Colors

Across
3. gray
6. earring
7. pants
8. blue
12. sock
14. coat
17. jacket
18. vest
20. red
21. handbag
22. glove

Down
1. glasses
2. hanger
3. yellow
4. orange
5. jeans
7. hat
9. purple
10. skirt
11. necklace
13. swimsuit
15. color
16. pink
18. white
19. shoe

No. 48
People

Across
1. hairdresser
3. fisherman
5. son
6. lawyer
9. mechanic
11. painter
12. woman
14. girl
16. aunt
17. judge
18. plumber

Down
2. sister
4. singer
7. man
8. pilot
10. farmer
11. mother
12. friend
13. hunter
15. cousin

No. 49
Actions

Across
3. to laugh
7. to point
8. to lick
9. to sneeze
10. to smile
13. to rub
15. to smell
17. to yawn
18. to stand
19. to shout
20. to pull

Down
1. to shake
2. to sing
4. to turn
5. to grip
6. to sit
7. to wink
11. to listen
12. to kneel
14. to blink
16. to cough

No. 50
The Outdoors

Across
3. rainbow
5. beach
6. cloud
9. rain
10. hail
11. river
12. frost
14. hill
16. forest
17. cold
18. fog
19. lightning
20. snow

Down
1. sea
2. rainy
4. mountain
5. lake
6. wind
7. volcano
8. storm
11. cliff
12. flood
13. valley
15. ocean
16. desert

No. 51

Numbers

Across
1. eighteen
4. five
5. twelve
7. fifteen
8. thirty
10. twenty
13. nineteen
14. one hundred
16. three
17. zero

Down
2. one
3. eighty
4. fifty
5. two
6. four
8. thirteen
9. fourteen
11. eight
12. ten
13. nine
15. eleven

No. 52
Days and Months

Across
1. Sunday
3. January
6. December
9. June
11. March
13. Monday
15. April
16. Friday
17. February
18. Thursday

Down
2. November
4. August
5. September
7. May
8. Tuesday
10. Saturday
12. July
14. October

No. 53
Animals

Across
2. octopus
4. animal
9. chicken
10. duck
12. dog
13. fish
15. cow
17. monkey
19. swan
20. camel
21. goose

Down
1. whale
2. rabbit
3. goat
5. deer
6. pig
7. lizard
8. horse
11. turkey
14. ant
15. cat
16. sheep
18. mouse

No. 54
The Body

Across
5. eyebrow
6. back
7. toe
10. foot
11. throat
14. hand
15. knee
16. leg
18. arm
19. tongue
20. thigh
21. chest

Down
1. body
2. cheek
3. heart
4. thumb
8. elbow
9. mouth
11. skin
12. eye
13. stomach
15. jaw
17. nose
19. tooth
20. ear

No. 55
Food

Across
1. salt
2. pea
4. nut
6. cabbage
7. banana
10. fruit
11. butter
12. meat
14. coconut
15. cream
17. pepper
18. chicken

Down
1. mustard
3. candy
5. spinach
6. pumpkin
7. cauliflower
8. yoghurt
9. eggplant
13. icecream
14. cheese
16. flour

No. 56

The Home

Across
2. fork
6. garden
7. bathmat
9. brush
15. nail file
16. shampoo
17. cup
18. soap
19. door
20. handle

Down
1. furniture
3. bed
4. blanket
5. container
8. kitchen
10. power point
11. sofa
12. mattress
13. toothpaste
14. table
16. chair

No. 57
Clothes and Colors

Across
2. tie
5. red
7. vest
9. orange
11. scarf
13. glasses
17. bra
19. ring
20. dress

Down
1. boot
2. necklace
3. green
4. stocking
6. belt
8. color
10. yellow
11. black
12. hat
14. pink
15. purple
16. gray
17. hanger
18. pants

No. 58
People

Across
4. plumber
6. son
7. doctor
10. baby
11. mechanic
14. aunt
18. mother
19. lawyer
20. cousin

Down
1. painter
2. boy
3. grandfather
5. butcher
6. singer
8. dentist
9. pilot
12. friend
13. farmer
15. father
16. woman
17. man

No. 59
Actions

Across
2. to yawn
3. to talk
4. to pull
7. to rub
8. to dance
11. to shout
12. to kick
13. to kneel
15. to eat
16. to lick
17. to turn
18. to scream

Down
1. to cry
2. to walk
5. to listen
6. to lie
8. to drink
9. to stand
10. to touch
11. to smell
14. to bend

No. 60
The Outdoors

Across
3. cloud
5. rainy
8. mountain
9. hail
11. cold
12. desert
13. river
17. island
20. weather
21. valley

Down
1. sea
2. lake
3. waterfall
4. fog
6. rain
7. hill
8. lightning
10. stormy
11. coast
14. flood
15. beach
16. frost
18. storm
19. forest
20. wind

No. 61
General vocabulary

Across
2. vest
6. June
7. shirt
11. lemon
12. finger nail
14. watch
18. uncle
19. noodle
21. brush

Down
1. pants
2. forest
3. cousin
4. animal
5. March
8. stomach
9. necklace
10. ear
12. friend
13. cucumber
15. blue
16. hand
17. soldier
20. egg

No. 62

Across
3. to listen
7. spoon
9. ring
10. sponge
12. to bend
14. toe
16. sultana
17. belt
20. melon
22. to laugh

Down
1. grandfather
2. perfume
4. eleven
5. throat
6. animal
7. lung
8. chimney
11. waiter
13. aunt
15. bird
18. pink
19. son
21. egg

No. 63

Across
1. mouse
6. to punch
7. June
11. coat
13. refrigerator
14. chicken
15. beach
17. sponge
18. doctor
19. whale
20. sixty

Down
2. salt
3. to run
4. February
5. goat
8. hill
9. fisherman
10. fruit
11. mouth
12. sheet
15. scarf
16. blanket

No. 64

Across
1. sheet
6. cupboard
7. to rub
8. alarm clock
10. finger
13. goose
14. doctor
16. knife
19. four
20. red
22. grandfather
23. dog

Down
2. knee
3. snow
4. cream
5. hunter
9. yoghurt
10. hair dryer
11. fork
12. garden
15. to drink
17. plug
18. frost
21. foot

No. 65

Across
3. hail
5. storm
7. chair
9. September
13. April
15. orange
16. seven
17. head
18. bee
19. one
20. to walk

Down
1. tap
2. snow
4. to turn
5. shorts
6. May
8. to lick
10. bread
11. to grip
12. fourteen
14. egg
15. uncle
16. to stand

No. 66

Across
1. to touch
3. mustard
5. curtain
6. hairdresser
7. coast
9. two
11. to drink
12. apple
13. April
16. watch
18. sofa
20. to grip
21. goat

Down
2. butterfly
4. cliff
7. plumber
8. hat
10. throat
14. fence
15. tongue
17. May
19. hair dryer

No. 67

Across
1. light
3. to dance
7. to eat
9. spinach
10. bear
12. stove
14. hip
16. towel
19. elbow
20. to kneel
21. three

Down
2. capsicum
4. toothbrush
5. octopus
6. earring
8. bowl
9. to scream
11. cave
13. kitchen
15. cucumber
17. hallway
18. yellow

No. 68

Across
1. toe
4. ring
7. to laugh
11. vegetable
12. to whisper
14. five
15. mouse
16. lake
17. table
20. purple
21. pink
22. Saturday

Down
2. hail
3. roof
5. tweezers
6. color
8. monkey
9. fifty
10. desert
12. hairdresser
13. nut
18. honey
19. blue

No. 69

Across
1. Friday
5. arm
7. tie
9. mirror
11. container
12. honey
14. plum
17. ten
18. icecream
19. lake
20. salt

Down
2. cake
3. cat
4. apple
6. back
8. kettle
10. hanger
12. throat
13. four
15. driver
16. white

No. 70

Across
5. singer
6. vegetable
8. dress
11. butter
13. sock
16. frost
19. seventy-eight
20. cave
21. hail

Down
1. island
2. alarm clock
3. desert
4. eighty-six
7. coat
9. thumb
10. fish
12. sheep
14. home
15. gate
17. chair
18. whale

No. 71

Across
1. color
4. pea
6. flood
7. butcher
11. window
12. curtain
15. snake
17. crab
20. dining room
21. three
22. eight

Down
1. hallway
2. chest
3. butter
4. duck
5. handle
8. green
9. to cough
10. to rub
13. back
14. yoghurt
16. noodle
17. cold
18. sauce
19. purple

No. 72

Across
3. bowl
7. to bend
8. juice
9. sea
12. twenty-four
14. eleven
15. nine
17. twenty
18. cucumber
20. candy
21. bird

Down
1. mustard
2. baby
4. eggplant
5. hair
6. vegetable
8. seventy
10. five
11. dog
12. fourteen
13. uncle
16. ocean
19. ring

No. 73

Across
1. eighty
4. eighteen
6. hairdresser
7. fence
8. September
11. to hold
13. to drink
15. to kneel
16. river
18. mirror
19. ant

Down
1. April
2. goose
3. heart
5. cake
6. Friday
9. Monday
10. garden
12. jeans
14. bee
17. purple

No. 74

Across
3. swimsuit
6. shirt
7. plug
9. waiter
10. lip
12. stormy
14. gate
15. cold
16. pasta
17. sleep
18. bowl

Down
1. container
2. to talk
4. monkey
5. fog
8. capsicum
10. to smile
11. belt
12. sponge
13. fifty
16. nut

No. 75

Across
1. Saturday
4. river
5. October
8. door
9. red
11. saucepan
14. bath
16. white
17. stairs
18. soup
19. seven
20. cucumber
21. waterfall

Down
2. microwave
3. butter
4. woman
6. bed
7. light
10. man
12. to hold
13. December
15. toe
16. vest

No. 76

Across
3. juice
4. tooth
5. dining room
7. fish
10. saucepan
11. goose
12. to talk
15. red
17. February
18. sock
19. back

Down
1. hunter
2. to look
3. seventy
6. pepper
7. finger
8. dog
9. spider
13. chest
14. knife
16. animal

No. 77

Across
2. tongue
4. cabbage
5. ring
8. mirror
10. ninety
11. yellow
12. to sing
14. tomato
16. brown
17. toaster
18. pilot
19. father

Down
1. to look
2. tongs
3. stairs
6. volcano
7. to blink
9. lizard
11. garden
13. lawyer
15. furniture

No. 78

Across
1. room
2. perfume
6. pea
9. fruit
11. nut
13. fourteen
15. kitchen
17. cheek
20. fork
21. gray

Down
1. forty-two
3. eighty-eight
4. river
5. trash can
7. sofa
8. cousin
10. uncle
12. mustard
14. fifty
16. hail
18. one
19. woman

No. 79

Across
6. one hundred
7. fish
8. arm
9. gold
12. glasses
16. stove
17. tap
18. lamp
20. plate
21. pea
22. ring

Down
1. Monday
2. hair dryer
3. animal
4. toe
5. finger
10. knife
11. Sunday
12. container
13. goose
14. ninety
15. toaster
19. sea

No. 80

Across
1. to dance
5. tongue
6. pants
7. stove
8. hat
12. nut
13. January
17. oven
18. handbag
20. ninety
21. waiter

Down
2. to pull
3. cabbage
4. handkerchief
5. toe
9. animal
10. to push
11. window
14. bed
15. floor
16. garage
19. blanket

No. 81

Across
1. nose
8. skirt
10. nail file
11. glass
12. spinach
14. red
18. fruit
19. sink
20. bird

Down
2. pig
3. Thursday
4. jeans
5. lung
6. arm
7. gold
9. waiter
12. chair
13. daughter
15. tomato
16. to stand
17. volcano

No. 82

Across
4. farmer
5. roof
7. stocking
10. gray
11. melon
14. bee
15. snake
17. to pull
20. ninety-nine

Down
1. foot
2. bread
3. comb
6. plum
8. ring
9. to talk
12. toe
13. plain
14. candy
16. to walk
18. wind
19. deer

No. 83

Across
1. Saturday
7. garden
8. gold
9. arm
11. thumb
13. to scream
16. shampoo
18. leg
19. January
20. stairs
22. white
23. frying pan

Down
2. bedroom
3. glass
4. mustard
5. stocking
6. purple
10. skirt
12. to walk
14. cloud
15. pea
17. painter
21. red

No. 84

Across
1. ten
3. hand
4. to scream
7. ninety
11. to push
14. forest
18. fish
19. jam
20. bee

Down
1. toe
2. boy
3. chicken
5. deer
6. goat
7. nose
8. face
9. son
10. power point
12. to run
13. storm
15. cream
16. lung
17. gray

No. 85

Across
3. mattress
7. fireplace
8. pants
10. spinach
11. to talk
13. twelve
14. honey
15. light
16. back
17. foot
18. tooth
19. fish
20. fog

Down
1. comb
2. forty-nine
4. swan
5. goose
6. bed
9. perfume
12. cloud
13. fence
14. hot
15. to laugh

No. 86

Across
2. kitchen
4. pants
6. son
7. eye
8. coast
10. plate
11. eight
13. underwear
14. dining room
19. February
20. noodle

Down
1. to walk
3. to eat
5. balcony
8. octopus
9. to swim
12. heart
15. shoe
16. pink
17. monkey
18. gray

No. 87

Across
1. monkey
5. furniture
8. farmer
11. pillow
14. to talk
16. December
18. storm
19. rice
21. to walk
22. potato

Down
2. foot
3. pea
4. skin
6. to run
7. mother
9. bean
10. to sing
12. mirror
13. cupboard
15. shower
17. bird
20. sheep

No. 88

Across
1. heart
3. skin
5. cheek
7. cloudy
9. foot
10. throat
11. wind
12. kitchen
13. hail
17. to bend
18. to lie
19. to push
20. gate

Down
2. fifty-two
3. hot
4. toaster
6. sofa
8. coast
13. pants
14. fork
15. glasses
16. face

No. 89

Across
1. hallway
2. octopus
4. May
7. razor
8. thumb
12. sock
13. bed
16. pale green
17. four
18. hair dryer

Down
1. finger
3. tie
4. Monday
5. to bend
6. cherry
9. monkey
10. back
11. sponge
13. farmer
14. to listen
15. July
16. bear

Across
1. bedroom
7. to sneeze
8. forest
11. October
12. spoon
14. jeans
16. bathroom
19. goat
20. tongue

Down
1. bowl
2. heart
3. man
4. spider
5. blanket
6. painter
9. red
10. plum
13. capsicum
15. pear
16. mountain
17. one
18. flour

No. 91

Across
2. grandfather
6. hot
7. crab
8. flour
9. to shake
11. fifteen
13. tap
15. sofa
18. oven
20. four
21. necklace
22. shower

Down
1. skirt
3. cup
4. to talk
5. to pull
9. sleep
10. valley
11. river
12. green
14. pants
16. color
17. nose
19. one

No. 92

Across
1. driver
7. toe
8. curtain
9. to cough
11. to eat
14. nose
15. bed
17. soap
18. sugar
20. tooth
21. cucumber
22. mother

Down
2. eighty-eight
3. fourteen
4. lung
5. blanket
6. judge
10. son
12. sixteen
13. eight
15. bear
16. white
19. comb

No. 93

Across
2. door
3. Friday
6. to smile
7. November
9. cauliflower
11. chicken
12. spinach
15. watch
16. wind
17. icecream

Down
1. lawyer
2. stairs
3. fish
4. vest
5. beach
8. volcano
9. butter
10. girl
12. sofa
13. cake
14. eye

No. 94

Across
1. hail
3. glasses
4. kitchen
8. soap
9. face
10. wall
11. to smile
13. camel
17. policeman
18. brown
19. grape

Down
2. to lick
3. mountain
4. handle
5. red
6. uncle
7. wind
8. power point
12. to blink
14. pea
15. four
16. cup

No. 95

Across
1. bath
4. red
6. bee
9. volcano
10. dog
12. melon
14. boy
15. island
16. eight
17. fork
18. toaster

Down
1. cauliflower
2. thirteen
3. hunter
5. cloudy
6. leg
7. fifty
8. cucumber
11. ant
13. mountain
14. jeans

No. 96

Across
1. laundry
3. yellow
5. glove
7. Saturday
8. honey
10. tongs
11. jacket
14. bowl
15. to sneeze
16. mountain
17. fisherman
18. tomato

Down
2. swan
4. purple
6. hot
7. to look
9. to laugh
12. knee
13. February
14. to sing
16. bread

No. 97

Across
3. to run
5. white
7. forest
8. kitchen
11. sixty
12. vegetable
13. woman
14. mirror
17. to kick
19. blender

Down
1. tongs
2. foot
4. light
6. pea
8. knee
9. glove
10. hanger
13. flood
14. son
15. ring
16. hair
18. rice

No. 98

Across
1. weather
4. light
8. one hundred
10. knee
12. animal
13. to cry
16. pig
18. monkey
19. hanger
20. singer
21. soldier

Down
2. to kick
3. blue
5. melon
6. seventy
7. bed
9. hot
10. pumpkin
11. blanket
14. balcony
15. to laugh
17. hail

No. 99

Across
1. five
3. nose
4. bird
5. head
6. to kneel
9. tomato
11. fruit
12. to point
13. bracelet
15. valley
16. twelve
17. yellow
19. garden
21. orange

Down
1. twenty-five
2. sock
5. necklace
7. dining room
8. May
10. toilet
14. shower
18. bear
20. egg

Across
4. hand
7. nineteen
8. bee
9. to lie
10. baby
11. vest
16. chicken
17. container
19. home
20. storm
21. to cough
22. thirteen

Down
1. goat
2. crib
3. flour
5. April
6. pepper
12. shoe
13. jaw
14. gray
15. thumb
18. noodle
19. tooth

No. 101

Across
1. bean
5. light
6. banana
9. arm
11. soup
13. cousin
15. oven
16. finger
18. wallet
21. four
22. garage

Down
1. brown
2. carrot
3. apple
4. hairdresser
7. eye
8. one hundred
10. head
12. gate
14. ninety
17. to lick
19. pink
20. egg

No. 102

Across
1. fruit
3. frost
7. cow
8. bathroom
9. to sit
12. mattress
15. brush
16. shoe
18. bed
20. animal
21. sleep

Down
2. farmer
3. river
4. man
5. seven
6. six
10. sneaker
11. yellow
12. knife
13. forty
14. to kick
17. cake
19. whale

No. 103

Across
2. curtain
4. coat
5. toaster
9. fork
10. blue
11. to sing
12. toilet
15. alarm clock
16. cup
18. honey

Down
1. gray
2. volcano
3. blanket
6. plate
7. fruit
8. rabbit
11. mirror
13. cake
14. twenty
15. weather
17. shoe

No. 104

Across
3. mother
7. wallet
9. pear
10. comb
12. nose
15. rice
16. pumpkin
17. to eat
19. candy
20. jacket
21. rain

Down
1. chicken
2. thumb
3. flour
4. door
5. saucepan
6. whale
8. ant
10. body
11. pants
13. Sunday
14. October
18. mustard

No. 105

Across
1. rainbow
2. shower
5. roof
6. frost
7. fruit
11. island
13. sofa
15. wind
16. pear
18. weather
19. June
20. finger

Down
1. deer
3. shorts
4. eight
8. black
9. fish
10. room
12. lung
14. earring
16. farmer
17. fence
18. white

No. 106

Across
2. ant
4. daughter
5. painter
7. October
9. March
10. waiter
11. stomach
13. cave
15. to lie
17. August
18. noodle
19. to hold

Down
1. pink
2. doctor
3. father
6. lamp
8. jaw
12. to turn
13. honey
14. to blink
16. fish

No. 107

Across
1. sock
6. skin
7. to look
10. door
11. foot
12. to turn
13. to whisper
15. three
17. onion
20. sponge
21. lake
22. cheek
23. stomach

Down
2. fruit
3. pepper
4. to hold
5. stormy
8. bracelet
9. noodle
14. seventy
16. skirt
18. one
19. to run

No. 108

Across
2. shower
7. fireplace
9. brown
10. to run
11. dishwasher
14. duck
16. pilot
17. wall
19. hunter
20. to listen

Down
1. furniture
3. hand
4. octopus
5. tweezers
6. frog
8. apple
9. floor
11. son
12. Wednesday
13. elbow
15. bath
18. gray

No. 109

Across
1. sleep
3. pea
6. mustard
7. octopus
9. to walk
10. six
11. door
12. meat
14. ceiling
16. doctor
18. Monday
19. glass
20. garage

Down
2. to cough
4. sheep
5. pepper
7. coast
8. waiter
10. to look
13. sailor
15. orange
17. sugar

No. 110

Across
1. sleep
3. Saturday
6. oven
8. monkey
13. glasses
14. sixteen
15. shirt
17. brown
20. grape
22. goose
23. ring

Down
2. fifteen
4. furniture
5. doctor
7. fish
8. bracelet
9. bathtub
10. dress
11. goat
12. six
16. coat
18. glass
19. leg
21. bear

No. 111

Across
1. shoulder
3. October
6. sleep
7. octopus
8. sofa
10. jeans
11. to lick
15. whale
16. Tuesday
17. juice
18. plug
19. bath
20. two

Down
2. hat
4. earring
5. fireplace
8. sultana
9. grape
12. tie
13. mustard
14. to sit

No. 112

Across

2. to scream
4. thumb
8. to whisper
9. waiter
10. sixty
14. bee
15. April
17. hair dryer
18. to touch

Down

1. oven
2. cupboard
3. brown
4. shower
5. March
6. flour
7. gate
11. to hold
12. garden
13. jaw
14. pear
16. dog

No. 113

Across
2. ant
4. twelve
5. saucepan
7. to stand
10. blanket
11. octopus
14. table
17. red
18. garage
21. throat
22. green

Down
1. sixty-nine
3. onion
6. jacket
8. Friday
9. juice
12. eighteen
13. brush
15. tooth
16. man
19. doctor
20. one

No. 114

Across
1. five
3. sheet
8. juice
10. August
11. goose
13. plumber
14. boot
16. to sneeze
17. fireplace
18. October
19. four
20. April

Down
2. flood
4. knee
5. storm
6. fifty-nine
7. to sit
9. finger
12. two
13. handle
15. alarm clock
17. dress

No. 115

Across
1. duck
5. comb
6. turkey
7. bean
12. handkerchief
15. lizard
18. mustard
19. judge
20. to touch

Down
2. table
3. father
4. son
5. knee
7. bed
8. glasses
9. five
10. scarf
11. June
13. to turn
14. to walk
16. cave
17. one

No. 116

Across
1. forest
5. bracelet
6. ten
8. to touch
12. fifty
13. duck
14. white
16. chimney
19. fence
20. sheet
21. glove

Down
1. wind
2. to punch
3. jacket
4. waterfall
6. tongue
7. Thursday
9. pig
10. doctor
11. eye
15. flour
17. to talk
18. lake

No. 117

Across
1. shirt
6. plate
7. brush
9. cousin
11. sauce
12. knife
13. color
15. lip
17. stocking
18. hail
19. one
20. curtain
21. refrigerator

Down
2. sailor
3. ear
4. wardrobe
5. plug
8. hunter
10. mountain
13. window
14. alarm clock
16. volcano

No. 118

Across

7. tomato
9. mustard
10. seven
12. foot
15. roof
16. eye
17. pasta
20. wardrobe
22. green

Down

1. color
2. tongs
3. cabbage
4. rice
5. bean
6. cup
8. eighty-eight
11. floor
13. wind
14. noodle
18. perfume
19. baby
20. to kneel
21. cold

No. 119

Across
3. stairs
6. rice
7. hip
9. goose
10. toilet
12. baby
13. sofa
16. face
17. June
18. horse
19. lip

Down
1. knife
2. four
4. room
5. lung
7. dog
8. curtain
11. twenty
13. scarf
14. wind
15. eye

No. 120

Across
2. fish
4. pink
5. April
8. camel
11. boot
12. flour
13. to eat
15. fence
17. light
18. island
20. oven
21. sultana
22. eleven
23. gate

Down
1. skirt
2. flood
3. sixteen
6. back
7. toilet
9. mother
10. rainbow
14. vegetable
16. soap
19. to lie

No. 121

Across
1. nose
3. soup
5. scarf
6. garage
8. spinach
9. color
10. soap
11. blanket
14. forty
15. father
17. to turn
18. shirt
19. February

Down
2. sofa
3. six
4. banana
7. bathmat
11. three
12. handle
13. onion
16. bee

No. 122

Across
1. fruit
4. mustard
5. glass
6. chicken
7. to shout
9. bracelet
12. toe
13. storm
15. sixty
17. swan
18. flood
19. perfume

Down
1. oven
2. animal
3. mouse
4. bedroom
5. goose
8. toothpaste
10. pasta
11. July
13. snow
14. deer
16. gold

No. 123

Across
1. apple
5. one
9. to bend
10. yellow
12. seventy-one
13. door
14. Sunday
18. cliff
19. frost
20. grape

Down
2. to lie
3. man
4. to wink
6. hip
7. eyebrow
8. valley
11. toothbrush
15. orange
16. pants
17. oven
18. foot

No. 124

Across
1. red
3. stocking
8. twenty-nine
12. twelve
13. to talk
15. hand
17. sheet
19. sugar
20. to taste
21. yellow
22. to shout

Down
2. orange
4. policeman
5. twenty-one
6. tongue
7. juice
9. to point
10. eggplant
11. oven
14. nineteen
16. cloud
18. cow

No. 125

Across
5. to wink
8. tooth
9. pasta
10. to eat
12. toilet
14. Monday
17. to scream
19. cave
22. judge
23. cheese

Down
1. purple
2. orange
3. eye
4. leg
6. thirty
7. towel
8. tongs
11. mother
13. cup
15. oven
16. white
18. hair
20. throat
21. flour

No. 126

Across
1. cloudy
2. fork
4. river
7. knife
9. tweezers
11. watch
13. ear
15. to rub
16. doctor
17. eighteen
18. milk

Down
1. forest
2. to yawn
3. to whisper
5. floor
6. father
8. stormy
9. pilot
10. skin
12. banana
14. necklace

No. 127

Across
8. to smell
9. sixty
10. foot
11. garage
13. January
15. butcher
18. blue
19. flood
21. woman
22. orange

Down
1. tap
2. driver
3. bottom
4. frying pan
5. rice
6. toe
7. handle
12. to walk
14. to rub
16. cucumber
17. noodle
20. door

No. 128

Across
1. Monday
5. to rub
6. doctor
7. to lick
8. eyebrow
10. to walk
13. one
14. fish
17. sugar
18. garage
19. knee

Down
2. ninety-eight
3. cabbage
4. underwear
5. back
8. August
9. to talk
11. hand
12. fruit
15. rain
16. glass

No. 129

Across
1. storm
5. monkey
7. April
10. spoon
11. eleven
14. crib
16. one
18. hill
19. fog
20. to drink

Down
1. beach
2. mouse
3. ceiling
4. banana
6. fork
8. lip
9. oven
12. cousin
13. sixty
14. handle
15. melon
17. fruit

No. 130

Across
1. shampoo
7. to dance
9. coat
10. eight
14. ring
16. cabbage
17. doctor
18. lizard
20. ocean
21. curtain

Down
2. chicken
3. October
4. hair dryer
5. six
6. meat
8. dishwasher
11. to stretch
12. swan
13. to shake
15. garden
16. to kneel
19. hot

No. 131

Across
1. wardrobe
7. Tuesday
9. home
11. thirty
13. lightning
15. girl
16. lung
17. two
18. eggplant

Down
2. island
3. sofa
4. monkey
5. kitchen
6. dress
7. thumb
8. shirt
9. onion
10. apple
12. ninety
14. to dance
15. painter

No. 132

Across
1. girl
3. bread
5. sponge
8. forest
9. brush
10. February
13. glove
16. shirt
18. hair dryer
19. pants
20. four
21. bird

Down
2. cave
4. October
6. mouse
7. jam
9. bear
11. sheep
12. coat
14. throat
15. honey
17. sea

No. 133

Across
4. roof
7. desert
8. orange
10. nineteen
11. pig
15. shower
18. body
20. light
21. pale green

Down
1. vegetable
2. father
3. shorts
5. butcher
6. curtain
9. pasta
11. sofa
12. stove
13. brother
14. doctor
16. sauce
17. hail
19. blue

No. 134

Across
4. white
6. to eat
7. cherry
10. wind
11. sea
12. towel
16. perfume
19. pilot
20. pale green

Down
1. nineteen
2. deer
3. to point
4. desert
5. meat
8. to hold
9. tomato
10. alarm clock
13. eighty
14. butter
15. to pull
17. mouse
18. skirt

No. 135

Across
1. gold
2. kitchen
4. Monday
5. salt
6. six
8. brush
10. pepper
12. to pull
13. hat
14. to sit
16. apple
17. boy
18. hair
19. gate

Down
1. vegetable
3. orange
7. seven
9. son
11. fifteen
12. toe
14. soldier
15. cucumber

No. 136

Across
2. pumpkin
5. shower
6. desert
8. two
10. cabbage
11. chest
13. shampoo
15. July
16. one hundred
19. arm
20. singer
21. container

Down
1. face
3. red
4. soup
5. roof
7. elbow
9. pink
12. sultana
14. Monday
16. to eat
17. to listen
18. April

No. 137

Across
1. to lick
5. eleven
8. light
9. two
12. foot
13. red
14. underwear
16. sponge
19. to look
21. ceiling
22. towel

Down
2. egg
3. comb
4. fog
6. grape
7. yoghurt
8. spoon
10. cloud
11. doctor
15. shirt
17. hand
18. May
20. bed

No. 138

Across
2. mouth
3. thirteen
6. hair dryer
7. six
10. toothpaste
12. fog
13. December
15. to dance
17. volcano
20. ocean
21. lake
22. cucumber

Down
1. rice
2. mouse
4. to shout
5. purple
8. dog
9. to point
11. door
14. sea
16. August
18. apple
19. sauce

No. 139

Across
1. cloudy
5. nut
8. elbow
9. bottom
12. cold
13. thirteen
15. skirt
16. to shout
17. hat
18. sea
19. sauce
20. dress
21. hot

Down
2. to run
3. wallet
4. baby
6. mirror
7. mustard
10. cream
11. shorts
13. roof
14. home
18. milk

No. 140

Across
1. hallway
4. yellow
7. flood
8. wind
9. beach
11. to sit
13. boy
15. trash can
16. color
18. roof
19. bean
20. lawyer
21. cold
22. ninety-three

Down
2. to run
3. farmer
5. lung
6. glass
10. turkey
11. sink
12. soap
14. eleven
17. eight

No. 141

Across
1. crab
7. to scream
9. shower
10. plate
11. pea
13. hairdresser
17. lizard
18. heart
19. oven
20. nine
21. green

Down
1. cow
2. to taste
3. mouth
4. glass
5. waiter
6. to grip
8. chimney
12. soup
14. cupboard
15. jaw
16. to talk

No. 142

Across
3. twelve
5. pear
8. to yawn
10. to pull
12. to laugh
14. vest
15. deer
18. door
20. elbow
21. lip
22. window

Down
1. to lie
2. to rub
4. lung
6. blender
7. hunter
9. actor
10. toe
11. man
13. icecream
16. chair
17. cloud
19. head

No. 143

Across
1. toaster
5. throat
6. tooth
7. balcony
9. to wink
10. mustard
14. light switch
16. tongue
17. ten
20. jam
21. salt
22. bed
23. fruit

Down
2. son
3. camel
4. bathroom
8. island
11. cheese
12. crib
13. green
15. comb
18. fog
19. bread

No. 144

Across
1. jacket
4. pants
7. roof
8. hallway
9. bean
11. August
12. Wednesday
15. cup
18. orange
19. to run
20. plug

Down
2. cabbage
3. kitchen
5. Sunday
6. pumpkin
7. three
8. fifty
10. necklace
11. eight
13. to hold
14. to lick
16. shoe
17. goose

No. 145

Across

2. October
4. oven
6. spider
8. yellow
10. gold
11. fence
12. chair
14. necklace
17. forty-five
18. May
19. pear

Down

1. pants
2. uncle
3. forty-one
5. hot
7. rain
8. gray
9. to cough
11. dentist
13. hat
15. to grip
16. July
17. woman

No. 146

Across
1. black
4. cat
5. ten
6. bread
9. purple
10. red
12. back
16. thirty
17. horse
18. mirror
19. turkey

Down
2. chicken
3. laundry
5. room
6. bean
7. door
8. garage
11. ear
13. nineteen
14. bee
15. to lie

No. 147

Across
3. to hold
5. to shake
7. cake
8. April
9. to wink
14. bath
15. gate
16. to cry
17. to bend
18. friend
19. spoon

Down
1. chocolate
2. shirt
4. animal
6. fence
10. waterfall
11. cow
12. to drink
13. window
15. horse
16. cheek

No. 148

Across
3. chest
4. hair
8. yoghurt
9. girl
10. July
14. orange
17. icecream
19. lounge room
20. fourteen
21. bath

Down
1. tongue
2. woman
5. eggplant
6. glasses
7. sock
11. bee
12. head
13. fence
15. to walk
16. cupboard
18. Monday
19. wall

No. 149

Across
3. skin
4. ten
5. storm
7. fifty-one
10. one
12. sister
15. vest
16. glass
19. melon
20. pasta
21. seventy

Down
1. bee
2. fireplace
5. singer
6. cup
8. fog
9. ear
11. to look
13. stairs
14. red
17. rice
18. June

No. 150

Across
1. Tuesday
5. swan
6. hanger
7. cup
8. light
12. stocking
14. frog
15. mustard
16. Sunday
18. back
19. fireplace

Down
1. roof
2. hip
3. juice
4. furniture
5. plug
9. apple
10. peach
11. twelve
13. to shout
16. son
17. arm

Antwort-Wörterbuch

actor	der Schauspieler	capsicum	der Paprika
alarm clock	der Wecker	carrot	die Karotte
animal	das Tier	cat	die Katze
ant	die Ameise	cauliflower	der Blumenkohl
apple	der Apfel	cave	die Höhle
April	April	ceiling	die Decke
arm	der Arm	chair	der Stuhl
artist	der Künstler	cheek	die Wange
August	August	cheese	der Käse
aunt	die Tante	cherry	die Kirsche
baby	das Baby	chest	die Brust
back	der Rücken	chicken	Hähnchen
balcony	der Balkon	chicken	das Huhn
banana	die Banane	chimney	der Schornstein
bath	das Bad	chocolate	die Schokolade
bathmat	die Badematte	cliff	der Felsen
bathroom	das Badezimmer	cloud	die Wolke
bathtub	die Badewanne	cloudy	wolkig
beach	der Strand	coast	die Küste
bean	die Bohne	coat	der Mantel
bear	der Bär	coconut	die Kokosnuss
bed	das Bett	cold	kalt
bedroom	das Schlafzimmer	color	die Farbe
bee	die Biene	comb	der Kamm
belt	der Gürtel	container	der Behälter
bird	der Vogel	cousin	der Cousin
black	schwarz	cow	die Kuh
blanket	die Decke	crab	der Krebs
blender	die Rührmaschine	cream	die Sahne
blue	blau	crib	das Kinderbett
body	der Körper	cucumber	die Gurke
boot	der Stiefel	cup	die Tasse
bottom	der Hintern	cupboard	der Schrank
bowl	Schüssel	curtain	der Vorhang
boy	der Junge	daughter	die Tochter
bra	der Büstenhalter	December	Dezember
bracelet	das Armband	deer	das Reh
bread	das Brot	dentist	der Zahnarzt
brother	der Bruder	desert	die Wüste
brown	braun	dining room	das Esszimmer
brush	die Bürste	dishwasher	die Spülmaschine
butcher	der Metzger	doctor	der Arzt
butter	die Butter	dog	der Hund
butterfly	der Schmetterling	door	die Tür
cabbage	der Kohl	dress	das Kleid
cake	die Torte	driver	der Fahrer
camel	das Kamel	duck	die Ente
candy	der Bonbon	ear	das Ohr

earring	der Ohrring	garage	die Garage
egg	das Ei	garden	der Garten
eggplant	die Aubergine	gate	die Pforte
eight	acht	girl	das Mädchen
eighteen	achtzehn	glass	das Glas
eighty	achtzig	glasses	die Brille
eighty-eight	achtundachtzig	glove	der Handschuh
eighty-six	sechsundachtzig	goat	die Ziege
elbow	der Ellbogen	gold	gold
eleven	elf	goose	die Gans
eye	das Auge	grandfather	der Großvater
eyebrow	die Augenbraue	grandmother	die Großmutter
face	das Gesicht	grape	die Weintraube
farmer	der Bauer	gray	grau
father	der Vater	green	grün
February	Februar	hail	der Hagel
fence	der Zaun	hair	das Haar
fifteen	fünfzehn	hair dryer	der Fön
fifty	fünfzig	hairdresser	der Friseur
fifty-nine	neunundfünfzig	hallway	der Flur
fifty-one	einundfünfzig	hand	die Hand
fifty-two	zweiundfünfzig	handbag	die Handtasche
finger	der Finger	handkerchief	das Taschentuch
finger nail	der Fingernagel	handle	die Klinke
fireman	der Feuerwehrmann	hanger	der Bügel
fireplace	der Kamin	hat	der Hut
fish	der Fisch	head	der Kopf
fisherman	der Fischer	heart	das Herz
five	fünf	hill	der Hügel
flood	die Flut	hip	die Hüfte
floor	der Boden	home	das Zuhause
flour	das Mehl	honey	der Honig
fog	der Nebel	horse	das Pferd
foot	der Fuß	hot	heiß
forest	der Wald	hunter	der Jäger
fork	die Gabel	icecream	die Eiscreme
forty	vierzig	island	die Insel
forty-five	fünfundvierzig	jacket	die Jacke
forty-nine	neunundvierzig	jam	die Marmelade
forty-one	einundvierzig	January	Januar
forty-two	zweiundvierzig	jaw	der Kiefer
four	vier	jeans	die Jeans
fourteen	vierzehn	judge	der Richter
Friday	Freitag	juice	der Saft
friend	der Freund	July	Juli
frog	der Frosch	June	Juni
frost	der Frost	kettle	der Wasserkessel
fruit	das Obst	kitchen	die Küche
frying pan	die Bratpfanne	knee	das Knie
furniture	die Möbel	knife	das Messer

lake	der See	orange	orange
lamp	die Lampe	oven	der Ofen
laundry	die Waschküche	painter	der Maler
lawyer	der Anwalt	pale green	blassgrün
leg	das Bein	pants	die Hose
lemon	die Zitrone	pasta	die Nudeln
light	die Lampe	pea	die Erbse
light blue	hellblau	peach	der Pfirsich
light switch	der Lichtschalter	pear	die Birne
lightning	der Blitz	pepper	der Pfeffer
lip	die Lippe	perfume	das Parfüm
lizard	die Eidechse	pig	das Schwein
lounge room	das Wohnzimmer	pillow	das Kopfkissen
lung	die Lunge	pilot	der Pilot
man	der Mann	pink	rosa
March	März	plain	das Flachland
mattress	die Matratze	plate	der Teller
May	Mai	plug	der Stöpsel
meat	das Fleisch	plum	die Pflaume
mechanic	der Mechaniker	plumber	der Klempner
melon	die Melone	policeman	der Polizist
microwave	die Mikrowelle	potato	die Kartoffel
milk	die Milch	power point	die Steckdose
mirror	der Spiegel	pumpkin	der Kürbis
Monday	Montag	purple	lila
monkey	der Affe	rabbit	das Kaninchen
mother	die Mutter	rain	der Regen
mountain	der Berg	rainbow	der Regenbogen
mouse	die Maus	rainy	regnerisch
mouth	der Mund	razor	der Rasierapparat
mustard	der Senf	red	rot
nail file	die Nagelfeile	refrigerator	der Eisschrank
necklace	die Kette	rice	der Reis
nine	neun	ring	der Ring
nineteen	neunzehn	river	der Fluss
ninety	neunzig	roof	das Dach
ninety-eight	achtundneunzig	room	das Zimmer
ninety-nine	neunundneunzig	sailor	der Matrose
ninety-three	dreiundneunzig	salt	das Salz
noodle	die Nudel	Saturday	Samstag
nose	die Nase	sauce	die Soße
November	November	saucepan	die Pfanne
nut	die Nuss	scarf	der Schal
ocean	der Ozean	sea	das Meer
October	Oktober	September	September
octopus	der Krake	seven	sieben
one	eins	seventeen	siebzehn
one hundred	einhundert	seventy	siebzig
onion	die Zwiebel	seventy-eight	achtundsiebzig
orange	die Orange	seventy-one	einundsiebzig

shampoo	das Shampoo	three	drei
sheep	das Schaf	throat	der Hals
sheet	das Laken	thumb	der Daumen
shirt	das Hemd	Thursday	Donnerstag
shoe	der Schuh	tie	die Krawatte
shorts	die Shorts	to bend	biegen
shoulder	die Schulter	to blink	blinken
shower	die Dusche	to cough	husten
singer	der Sänger	to cry	weinen
sink	das Waschbecken	to dance	tanzen
sink	das Spülbecken	to drink	trinken
sister	die Schwester	to eat	essen
six	sechs	to grip	greifen
sixteen	sechzehn	to hold	halten
sixty	sechzig	to kick	treten
sixty-nine	neunundsechzig	to kneel	knien
skin	die Haut	to laugh	lachen
skirt	der Rock	to lick	lecken
sleep	der Schlaf	to lie	liegen
slipper	der Hausschuh	to listen	hören
snake	die Schlange	to look	schauen
sneaker	der Turnschuh	to point	zeigen
snow	der Schnee	to pull	ziehen
soap	die Seife	to punch	schlagen
sock	die Socke	to push	schieben
sofa	das Sofa	to rub	reiben
soldier	der Soldat	to run	laufen
son	der Sohn	to scream	schreien
soup	die Suppe	to shake	schütteln
spider	die Spinne	to shout	rufen
spinach	der Spinat	to sing	singen
sponge	der Schwamm	to sit	sitzen
spoon	der Löffel	to smell	riechen
stairs	die Treppe	to smile	lächeln
stocking	der Strumpf	to sneeze	niesen
stomach	der Magen	to stand	stehen
storm	der Sturm	to stretch	strecken
stormy	stürmisch	to swim	schwimmen
stove	der Herd	to talk	reden
sugar	der Zucker	to taste	schmecken
sultana	die Sultanine	to touch	anfassen
Sunday	Sonntag	to turn	abbiegen
swan	der Schwan	to walk	gehen
swimsuit	der Badeanzug	to whisper	flüstern
table	der Tisch	to wink	zwinkern
tap	der Wasserhahn	to yawn	gähnen
ten	zehn	toaster	der Toaster
thigh	der Oberschenkel	toe	der Zeh
thirteen	dreizehn	toilet	die Toilette
thirty	dreißig	tomato	die Tomate

tongs	die Zange
tongue	die Zunge
tooth	der Zahn
toothbrush	die Zahnbürste
toothpaste	die Zahnpasta
towel	das Handtuch
towel rack	der Handtuchhalter
trash can	der Mülleimer
Tuesday	Dienstag
turkey	der Truthahn
tweezers	die Pinzette
twelve	zwölf
twenty	zwanzig
twenty-five	fünfundzwanzig
twenty-four	vierundzwanzig
twenty-nine	neunundzwanzig
twenty-one	einundzwanzig
two	zwei
uncle	der Onkel
underwear	die Unterwäsche
valley	das Tal
vegetable	das Gemüse
vest	die Weste
volcano	der Vulkan
waiter	der Kellner
wall	die Wand
wallet	die Brieftasche
wardrobe	der Kleiderschrank
watch	die Armbanduhr
waterfall	der Wasserfall
weather	das Wetter
Wednesday	Mittwoch
whale	der Wal
white	weiß
wind	der Wind
window	das Fenster
woman	die Frau
yellow	gelb
yoghurt	der Joghurt
zero	null